I0417555

The Myth
Of the Strong Black Woman

Ramona Lofton Wright

DEDICATION

I Dedicate this book to my husband Joseph, who was hurt and saddened by some of the content of this book, but who never the less approved of its publication and allowed me to vent and "air our dirty laundry" in a public setting. He did this in order for me to heal and put much of my anxiety behind me. My hope is that others will understand my writing and perhaps find a creative way to express their happiness, joy and pain.

I would also like to dedicate this book to myself because being able to express my pain and suffering has indeed been a cathartic, healing experience. I am so grateful that I allowed myself this outlet for creative expression.

Ramona Lofton Wright

ACKNOWLEDGEMENTS

Special acknowledgement must be paid to my mother Love Jordan Valadez, who read the bible to her children every night — giving us moral direction, teaching us to love Jehovah our God, giving us poetry, music, art, love and so much more. She gave us the tools to survive prejudice, unkindness and child abuse (even though she never realized it was happening right under her nose.)

To my daughters: Sylvia Hillman, a published author and screenwriter in her own right; Ramona Lisa Steele, who is an artist, poet, musician and my editor who directed me through the creative process of this book; Carmen, who will never read this book but who loves me and her father, and keeps up with our health and chauffeurs us to doctor's appointments and makes sure we have all that we need on a day to day basis; to John and Simon my prodigal sons, who are on beautiful paths back to soundness of mind and heart health.

To my life coach Dr. Landrum, who insisted I finish this book and publish it as part of my healing process.

FORWARD

MY PEN FLOWS

This silver Paper Mate pen feels so good in my hand, it just flows
Flows with poetry and prose
Flows with pain and sorrow
With hope for tomorrow
I know it's elementary, the things that I write, but I'm not writing for you
I'm writing for me and it makes me feel free to let my pen flow
Don't you know
It's fun because I can really mix it up and don't have to be graded by teachers or masters of the trade
I can say a riddle
Oh what a piddle
I can say a rhyme
In my good time
I don't have to have pitch, pace, power or tempo,
Like Thoreau (sp?)
Cuz, I don't want to
I can stop the scale on the sixth note and drive everyone crazy
Open-paren... smile... close-paren. Except me
Commas and punctuation correct? Forget it! Not wit it... come what may...
I'll say it my way dot dot dot

Ramona Lofton Wright

Note: These poems that I paint are my bag. After all, I'm an artist.

CONTENTS

LOVE, PAIN & SELF-PITY

ARE YOU MINE?

As we lay in the Kasbah, I say to my lover
Are you mine?
Oh, let me think he says
Yea! You do that I say
While I go to the potty
hee hee

Are you mine?
Like a fine wine
Don't bet a dime
You with your funny line

Are you mine? Till the end of time?
Now turn over and let me pat that hind
Yes, I'm yours – now do your chores and let's not snore

Be careful what you ask for

There must be a million poems, and songs written about it
Why is it such a hot topic? No doubt there is a problem with it
It's longed for by lovers, husbands and wives, girlfriends and boyfriends, bosses and workers
Everyone says they want it, must have it, but when they get it they hate it
It hurts, it stings, embarrasses, humiliates
Opens old wounds and happily creates new ones
It gashes open your heart to realities ugly and cruel
It forces you to do the math
Yes, be careful what you ask for you just might get it
Honestly, it's just plain honesty my friend

Betrayed by a Kiss

A sweet tender kiss right in the middle of my forehead
A sweet tender kiss to hide my sign

I feel so betrayed by that sweet tender kiss
Betrayed by the love of my life, by the man of my dreams... or is he?
Have my dreams changed over the years and become fodder for fools?
Have I fought the fine fight for nothing

Maybe I have. I feel that way now. Like a fool, for only fools fall in love. Maybe it's me that does not know how to love. If marriage is the union of two good forgivers, why must it be so painful?

My heart is heavy and weighed down. My heart hurts so badly that I wish I could cry, or die to lift the pain and anguish of mind body and soul.

Communication is the key they say, so I try once again —only to my surprise—only to my demise.

BLENDING

Blending two cultures
Two worlds
Blending two hearts
That so opposite attract

Please know, my love,
The older I get
The more I fear
The more insecure I feel in our love
The more hopelessness this crazy heart imagines
This sad heart stumbles forth with haphazard weariness, confused and dejected

Please know my dear I need to hear
Your comforting voice, your conversations of trust
Telling me again and again
How you feel
What you need
And that you love me for real

CAN OF WORMS

Boy did you ever open up a can of worms, slimy, snotty and tightly entangled, gross morose, inseparable yet somehow estranged.
What are we to do with this nasty can of worms my friend?
YUCK!!! Don't pour honey on it!

DANCE WITH ME

Dance with me baby,
Step with me tonight,
Hold me right, hold me tight

Slip your powerful arms around my waist
Pull me close to you

And sway with me
Stroll with me
Skip with me
Dip with me

Dance with me baby, it's Monday night

DEPRESSION

Depression is an enemy in this world of confusion
It attacks like any other disease, slowly and sneaky you don't even know it's there before it
pounces on you and drives you mad from within
For years, we knew not what it was, but now we have help, all kinds of help

Thanks for the medication
Thanks for the friends
Thanks for the encouragement
That never will end

Thanks for the understanding of what's really going on
And thanks for the mainstay of daily prayer

For Jah is with us to the very end
And soon depression we'll no more contend

Do the Math!

Got to clean it up man, this mess that you made, these eyes that you fade
Got to clean it up man, this heart that you broke, this throat that you choke
Got to clean it up man, this pain that you gain the brain that you strain
Got to clean it up man, this trust that you lost this anger you boss
Head pounding, ears ringing, eyes swollen, chest aching, fingers trembling, legs pacing,
stomach in knots because of those thoughts.

Even Though

(Pr 19:14)   The inheritance from a father is a house and wealth, but a discreet wife is from Jehovah.

Even though you don't love me no more
I will not be the one to walk out the door
I will not be the one to pack and leave
For that's what Satan wants to achieve

A way to hack
A way to chip and swing at the loyalty we promised
To destroy the integrity Jah admonished
Even though you don't want to do right
I won't be the one to take flight!
For Hope Burns Ever Bright!

FRIENDS OLD AND NEW

Our hope, on the evening of this, our 21st wedding anniversary, is that you eat good food, enjoy the best association and entertainment in town.

Laugh with us and be happy. Dance with us and get those endorphins pumping. When you go home tonight, get a good night's sleep and be refreshed for another spiritual day of activity in Jehovah's Service.

May Jehovah bless you with a joyful heart. Whatever problem you have now, it is no problem if you are friends and servants of Jehovah. I mean really now, what will it matter in a hundred years?

GRIEF! SHUT UP AND LET HIM TALK
Inspired by Mike Lofton (thanks Mike)

Why can't I shut up and let my man talk?
Let him tell me how he feels for a change
Is he happy, sad or even mad?
I don't need to describe or define his thoughts and intentions for him

Why can't I shut up and just let him talk?

Why do I need to feel the rush of my own lips, hurling, swirling, bubbling forth sounds so desperately...

Am I that insecure?
Why can't I shut up and not interrupt?

The muddle, the puddle I am trying to save him from
I'm already in

HONORED BY A KISS 🍎

A sweet tender kiss right in the middle of my forehead. A sweet tender kiss to chase away my fears. I feel so honored by that sumptuous tender kiss. Honored by the love of my life, by the man of my dreams... and he truly is.

No my dreams have not changed over the years and become fodder for fools. I did not fight the fine fight for nothing. I feel that way now. Vindicated by my lover for not only fools fall in love. Maybe it's me that does not know how to love. And since marriage is the union of two good forgivers, and a lack of communication can be so painful...

How grateful I am that I trusted my heart to my lover, my man, my husband.

For my heart is no longer heavy and weighed down. My heart no longer hurts so badly that I wish I could cry, or die to lift the pain and anguish of mind, body and soul.

Communication is the key for true lovers. It is worth all effort and pain. For to us we shall gain (through loyalty and heart) a sweet refrain.

How Does it Feel?

How does it make you feel, I really want to know
How does it make you feel to know you have us both
Does it make you feel like a big strong man, make you want to boast
Does your chest fill with pride, Hey look at me fellas
I got two women wanting me Two I say

Bright and intelligent, full of vigor and charm, grace and beauty
Oh and here's the best part, they got big bootys too

Yeah, they are fighting over me, what can I say
I mean, man I got it like that
Trying to make me choose one over the other? Please
Why should I bother, I got them both, I want them both, I love them both, I need them
both

One to stay home, take care of me, love me come hell or high water, take care of my
mother, scrub my back, rub my feet, clean my nails, wash my dog...call me a hog? I don't
care I'm gonna milk these cows for as long as they let me, cause I got two woman fighting
over me

One is willing to be my Mrs. Jones *we got a thing going on, we both know that it's wrong, but
it's much too strong to let it go... we meet every day at the same* time Monday thru Friday
4:30 in the morning. I listen to her sweet voice telling me what I want to hear. Like a drug
I'm soothed and calmed, wrapped up in the hypocrisy of her lie, mesmerized like a charmed
snake in a basket coming out to the magic of her flute. Like a beautiful song her voice is to
me. I wish I could take her and my wife and morph them together, have the best of both
worlds under one roof. Oh well.

Is that how you feel boy? Is that what you wish? Don't live in a dream world not willing to
face truth. A hurricane is coming to make Ivan look small, then you won't feel so tall.

I hear it coming now, I smell it in the air
I see it on the horizon coming like a mighty dust storm to swallow you up
I feel sorry for her, I feel sorry for you, I feel sorry for me cause we are not going to miss it.
It's pay the piper day
How does it feel boyee? Cuz man you ain't got it like that!

I DONE LOST MY MAN BLUES

As I wander through this maze of frustration and despair, I cry, I scream, I pray and hope... too much to dare

I can't believe it has happened to me, why would yet another man want to leave me? That man done lost his mind no doubt, for I am all that and a side of curly fries to boot

And yet
Here I am
Singing the "I done lost my man blues" again

I woke up this mornin'... dat da da da dat!
My man was not home... dat da da da dat!
I said I woke up this mornin'... dat da da da dat!
And that man had gone... dat da da da dat!
I looked out the window... dat da da da dat!
His truck was not there... dat da da da dat!
Yes I looked out my window... dat da da da dat!
But his truck it was gone... dat da da da dat!
Oh where could that man be... dat da da da dat!
Oh where could he be... dat da da da dat!
In the arms of another... dat da da da dat!
Cuz it sho' nuff ain't me... dat da da da dat!
He's not to be found... dat da da da dat!
Cuz he sho' nuff is gone, Yes he's not to be found, that man he done gon'
 dat da da da dat!

I done lost my main man... and that's just a shame
Yes it's just that
Oh yeah the blues done got me... and that's all she wrote

The next time I see's him...
It'll be all that he wrote (smile) te he he he he
Cuz he'll be the one that
Gonna get hisself smoked
Dat da da da dat!
Yes he gonna be the one, gonna get hisself broked

I LIKE HIM, HE DON'T LIKE ME, IT'S OVER

There is something worse than the torture of waiting for someone who said he'd call
There is something worse than the anguish of wondering will he want another date and won't be late
There is something worse than a hopeful fantasy: will he want me, will he want to emote and float with me, swing with me sway with me?
Something wonderful occurs when embracing the freeing reality of not wasting your time, or a dime on him
If I like him and he don't like me, we are free of frustration and lies, it's just over and you're free to move on to another one
One that will chase and send candy and flowers, will call on the hour and dime, are things of the past

I SEEN HIM

I seen him
Many a time
As that little box chimes with rhythm and rhyme
Lookin', peepin' and makin' up his mind
Should I answer
Should I not...
I seen him, many a time

I seen him look with disgust and disdain
Like whoever it was would give him a pain, make him insane
I seen him not answer, just put the phone down like they was nobody,
Not nothing, some clown

I seen him look happy and snappy and joyful when, someone he loves is on the line,
Someone he wants to talk to all the time (all day if he could, and he would)

I seen him look at that phone with fear and distrust when it rang like someone might catch
Him and trap him and scold him at best

So when I call, I'm not so surprised when he don't answer or pick up my line
You see, I can imagine the look on his face
Yep, I seen him

INTIMATE ENEMIES

Is that what we have become
Intimate enemies
How can you hate me yet make love to me so strongly
How can you neglect my mind, my thoughts, yet passion overflows in you behind closed doors
How can you look at me with disgust and disdain, yet lust after me all evening
What a shame
Have we become intimate enemies?
Let fix it
It's broken

Is He Afraid?

Is he afraid to come into our bedroom because he doesn't want to face me
Is he afraid to come into our bedroom because he doesn't want to hear my mouth
If only he knew I wasn't going to talk to him
He could come in here and play cards on the computer
He could come in here and look at TV
He could come in here and not worry tonight
Because I'm just too tired to tell him what he already knows

The lack of respect, the sneaky things he does
The lack of love, not caring if we live or die, if we serve Jah half-heartedly
Of if we serve him at all
I'm sick of blaming everything on Joe, it's really me and I know it
I think I'll just live my life in another part of the house
I would never dream of divorce but I dream of love

I would never leave him because there is always hope
That he will grow up one day and be the man that Jehovah
Wants him to be, the man that he wants to be, not afraid of confrontation
Always having Jehovah's back, Jesus' back, my back
Is he afraid of losing the love of his children?
Is he afraid of losing the love of his family? Does he care if he loses mine?
I wish I knew. He would say he is not, but his actions say something else

How I love him and wish him strength
Strength in Jehovah and our eternal future

How I want the very best for him, to learn not to be selfish, for he can be so giving to all
others, that don't really give a care – just fakin' and shakin' used by Satan as a snare.

Must I be taken for granted this late in life; did I do it again? Make another mistake?
How I long to love someone who loves Jehovah with all his soul, might and strength
Who loves Jehovah more then his genitals. Or mine.

LET'S FIX IT, WE ARE BROKEN
(Pr 18:15) 15

The heart of the understanding one acquires knowledge, and the ear of wise ones seek to find knowledge
We were two, then we were one, now we are two again
We are broken, we are sad, we are mad in our pad
Lets get back together as one
We are broken, we are sad, we are mad in our pad
Lets break open our old toolbox that we keep on that shelf
Lets dust it off, break it open and use those tools to fix us like new, not two
Let's fix it together
For we are broken

PRAYER FOR MY HUSBAND

I prayed for you today my darling, for you my dear heart
I prayed for you today my darling, morning, noon and night
I prayed to our God Jehovah that you would be honest and true
I prayed to our God to give you power beyond normal, and strength anew, to help you resist and desist from your wicked desires, to help your heart be complete toward those that you owe
I prayed for you my darling, my husband, my love
I prayed to our God Jehovah that you would fight the fine fight against him that is taunting, who is saying he got you and keeping you close, who says you love him the most and will obey with a thirst

Who will spit on Jah's promise and turn a deaf ear. Or fake it and smile with a twisted green glare.

Jah can't see me, who cares if he does, I'm having my fun now and play the game
Well, fix it later or do I dare

No let me stop now so my soul he won't hate, he won't take

I prayed for you my husband the love of my life to fight the fine fight the one that most matters the one that is noble, good, clean and just

To Jah unite your heart, your mind, body and soul, for Jah chose you first and to him you belong, don't let Satan steal you away from him
for he will for a certainty hurt you and trick you my love,
like it a moment or two, then desert you and laugh at our God in the end
don't let that come true don't do it my friend

I prayed for you my husband, my lover, my man, and wait ever hopeful your love to amend

SO TIRED... SO EMPTY

I'm so tired, so empty you say
Sorry boy. You got to give it up
You say so tired?
Tired of what?
You say you're so empty inside
When were you full?
You say you have nothing left to give
I say you have just begun
You say that I hurt you; you cannot forgive
Boy don't even go there, for I forgot how many times I forgave you and don't even remember what you did

You say you're so tired
Then take a vitamin
You say you're so empty
Then get a tank of spiritual gas
You say you have nothing left to give
Boy you are holding out. If you have it for her, it belongs to me. You are letting her steal what is not yours to give. So please just shut up!

SORRY

I'm so sorry that I can't stand you right now

I'm so sorry that you were unfaithful to me, to your vow, to our God

I'm so sorry that your heart is not devoted to mine, that we are not as one after all this time

I'm sorry that you could be dishonest with me, not trust in me, commitment is gone or was it ever in place, to efface, to erase

I'm sorry that our love did not last, that you put it away, that you dropped the ball, that you made us small

I'm so sorry for me and for you, that my man is lost, confused, bewildered, deceitful, selfish, disloyal and unkind, yes totally blind

I truly am sorry for our loss

Let's hope what was lost, can be found, before it is too late... So contemplate if you want to be my friend my man, my better half,

If not,

I'm so sorry,

That you're so sorry

The 20 Year Itch

(Pr 19:11) The insight of a man certainly slows down his anger, and it is beauty on his part to pass over transgression.

We used to joke, you and I, 20 years or so ago
We said we would turn each other in for two 20s when we turned 40
And even though you were tempted along the way
That never happened of course
I wondered what would happen when I went through the change but got through it with a little help from you and my friends
I was shocked and was reeling with feeling
I thought it would never happen to you babe
Not this Tower of Power
Not you, for you were my knight in shining armor, my savior from all kinds of pain, the one that could see deep inside of me (or so I thought)
Oh, but reality did rear its ugly head the day I found out you were human and had the same imperfections as all of Adam's children. How could I have been so wrong, so tricked and deceived by the illusion of the dream-man I created in my mind?
I blame you not, my love, for it was I, you see, living in my fantasy

The Morning After

This is the morning after
After he told me he was unfaithful in heart, mind and emotion
After he told me he didn't love me with passion
After he talked to the other
After he broke it off with her
After I told him I still love him
This is the morning after

THE TOUCH, THE LOOK, THE HOOK

The touch of his fingertips
How they ignite
The touch of his fingertips
How they excite
The look in his eyes
How they inspire
The look in his eyes
How they bring fire
The touch of his lips so firm and yet tender cause my
heart to melt, my soul to surrender
The touch
The look

I'm sorry to say that the hook he possesses has violently
pushed itself deep in my heart like a jelly fish, whose tentacles after slapping, attach
themselves to your flesh, thrust their razor sharp hooks in your skin. No, there's no pulling
them out, for like fish hooks they explode, tear and dig in deeper, and deeper until they
release their deadly venomous poison. Pumping it through the layers of flesh and muscle of
my heart. I am trapped and there is no antidote; the only relief from the searing pain is
death, sweet slumbering death.

I say once again no man can replace him no not this one... for only this man has that touch
of passionate poison.

the look
the hook

The Truth Will Set You Free

They say the truth will set you free but free to do what?
Make the same mistakes all over again
Companion of mine, why did you wait 20 years
If you know what you want and you are not getting what you want
then move on
If you know what you need and can't get it with speed
then move on
If you have what you want
If you have what you need
Then show me you do
Cuz I'm not chasing it
I'm not forcing it
And I'm not Feelin' it

To Love, Honor and Betray

They say to Love Honor and Betray is the norm for most marriages today.

What should I have done before I got married? Make a pros and cons list? Was loyalty a myth? Expected but not clarified? Insisted on but not communicated? A requirement of our commitment to our lifelong relationship, yet not in the pre-nup?

A bit too late, I dare say.

How many lies have there been between us? How long have you been leading a double life? Did you carve out a double heart at the start?

You are caught up and oh how it hurts. I hear you say, "I can't stop it, she's like a drug... yeah, I know it's wrong, but she makes me feel happy and strong, and so *so* good inside... I know, I know drugs are no good and bad, but I did stop weed eventually, remember?"

What you said hurt me no doubt, but you know what they say, to love honor and betray is the norm in most marriages today.

We Had It All

We had it all (with Jah's blessing to boot)
But we blew it my friend
On mere dust, flesh and loot...
Then your sin with death paid in full
Leaving me unfaithful to the test with no rest
Once again holding the bags in my rags
With no one to blame but my flesh, dust and loot

I grope for my reflection in the mirror of my sword
Hoping an ignorant woman deserving of pity looks back
Sad and mad, only a stupid one appears with no excuses only regrets

Pray now my new love and I n'er do the same
For tis he I now love
From deep trickling within
And tis that same love that may save or ruin
For again we have it all with Jah's blessing (to boot)

So I turn to our God with full heartfelt trust
And beg that he unify my tedious black treasonous heart to fear him and love him as I truly
want too; as I truly must
Save we pray, that our love is true
That our love for each other is pure through and through
Not the love of mere passion, lust and dust
But agape love from our God that as we trust

What's Up Baby

What's up baby, how you doing today
Are you happy
Are you sad
Are you up
Are you down
Tell me how you doing baby, so I can plan my day
Yea, you mean that much to me, the one that is worth my concern
You are the better portion of my heart, never to part

WHERE WOULD I BE IF I DIDN'T MARRY YOU?

I don't know, but I can imagine I would be married to someone else who was not in the truth when I met him at 1st but had bedroom eyes lowered at half-mast

Surely not kind, trustworthy or committed, but with firm, soft lips, dripping in honey

Not loyal, believable or faithful

But had a voice like Barry, make a girl wanna marry

Not humble or hungry for the truth, but with unbelievable strength and power in his arms, not wise but could mesmerize, not honest, won't treasure or cherish me, but knows just where to touch me, how hard, how soft, how slow, how fast, how shallow am I

Doesn't know a *good thang* or how to make it last or do the math

Where would I be if I didn't marry you?

Who knows, maybe in the nut house, in jail, or maybe dead?

If not, than looking, searching for a man, just like you, someone to hurt me, desert me.... inadvertently

WHO IS SHE BOY?
From a Hater (aka me)

Boy has you lost your mind?

Do you think I'm that stupid?

Do you think I don't see the loss of love in your eyes?

Do you think I don't see the hate in your sneer?

Do you think I don't see the grudges you carry

   ever since, we got married

Do you think I don't hear your sighs when I ask for a favor?

Who is she boy?

Who is she?

Boy has you lost your mind? Do you think I am that naive?

Do you think I do not feel the loss of magic in your touch?

Do you think I don't see how you hate to come home after work?

Do you think I don't see all the new friends you have, that you don't bring home but call on the phone?

Do you think I don't see the crazy phone bills we have?

Who is she boy?

Is she pretty? Is she is tight?

Does she got money?

A good job? Is that right?

Then give her your phone bill and see if she'll pay it

Cuz you crazy if you think I will, and she's double crazy if she thinks you will

WHY

Why do I want you

Is it because I can't have you

Is it because you don't want me

Is it because you fell so far out of love with me that I am invisible

Is it because I got fat

Is it because you lost interest

Is it because I am mean

Is it because I am pushy

Is it because I speak truth even when it hurts

Is it because we don't talk on the phone anymore

Someone else took that job

WILL HE STOP?

Does he have the power? Yes he does, but will he stop? Does he want to? No. Should he? Yes! But will he stop and make his heart whole again, complete and sound, not controlled by a creation, that's simply a puppet on a string herself, being used as bait, on a hook to tease, lure, tantalize and subdue him. She's a stranger.
A happy fool for one moment in time, not worth a dime.
Do the math, correct your path.

YOU'RE LAAAZY
(Pr 18:9) Also, the one showing himself slack in his work—he is a brother to the one causing ruin.

Man you're lazy
You give me a pain
You won't lift a finger
Unless it's to gain
If it's not pleasurable to you
Than it is forgotten, regardless of how it affects those who love you
But do they? How can they when it's not given back

Man you're lazy and driving me crazy
I think I will just let you go
And do whatever you do best
Ya do it, whatever I don't know
I don't care anymore
You're not worth all the tears that I cry
Pain you infuse
I will never be used. What you want – what you need to go do, do. Cause
You can't handle it any other way
Yes man, go do it
Cuz, man you are lazy

JOY, PATIENCE & APPRECIATION

BLONDIE

WOW!

My sister bleached my hair blond today
Ain't I cute?
I may be 58
I may be over weight
I may even be intimate friends with the Ritus Brothers But Boy oh Boy
Ain't I cute?

BRING ALL THE SUNSHINE IN

Come sunshine in all your glory, for today
is a day of release
Release from fear
Release from lack of understanding
A day of love and insight

It doesn't matter how hot it is because it is better than the bitterness and freezing
hopelessness of not knowing
Bring all the sunshine in
Oh happy day of release!

DOUBLE DUTCH

Big Black Skillets are always flyin
Jump boy jump boy or your cryin
Big Black Skillets are always flyin
Jump girl jump girl or you're diven
Big black skillets are always flyin
There goes daddy and I ain't lyin
Ah 1, Ah 2, Ah3

Hot skillet black skillet sittin on the stove
What you got cookin?
Nappy hair and bruising?
Ah 1, Ah 2, Ah 3

FILL YOUR HEART WITH GOOD THINGS

(Pr 20:5) Counsel in the heart of a man is as deep waters, but the man of discernment is one that will draw it up.

To fill my heart with good things is my goal, for it is full of bitterness and pain, malice and irritation enough to fill an ocean. To fill my heart with righteousness is my quest, for it is faulty and erroneous, ugly and felonious. To fill my heart with pleasantness is my goal, for it is treacherous and hopeless and cannot be trusted. To be loyal to my God is my desire, to make his heart rejoice when he gazes upon me with interest, looking for a reason to love me and protect me for my heart is useless and hopeless. To fill my heart with grace is my quest, for it is angry and unruly, unforgiving and just plain mad and sad, not happy joyful or glad. How wonderful to know I can choose to fill my heart with good things, to cherish and bless and not make yet another mess.

HAPPY DAY

(Pr 19:26) He that is maltreating a father [and] that chases a mother away is a son acting shamefully and disgracefully.

Oh what a happy day is today for mom is coming home from the hospital after a stroke.
I learned so much during these past five days.
I learned that it is not all about me and the injustices in the world.
It is about seeing someone precious gain her strength back, bit-by-bit, day-by-day.
It is about not losing a loved one and coming too close to death.
It is about seeing your prayers answered yet again when you get to bring your mom home from the hospital.

It is joy, not pain, because no matter what is inflicted upon you or what Satan attempts to do to get you to loose your integrity or be disloyal, something as fearful as losing a loved one can bring you back to the reality of everyday life. I do so love life and give it willingly on behalf of my God Jehovah, who, due to his loyal love, appreciates my lowly gift.

HOPE IS RENEWED

It's a new day
Or so they say
After struggling all night
To remain faithful and true
After fighting the
Fine Fight
In my mind
And heart

That vicious battle has once again
Been won

Hope is renewed and love restored
It's a new day I shout
Shout from the depths of my soul
From my very inner core

A new struggle to begin
Worth all the pain
For the honor to gain

INTEGRITY
TIL DEATH DO US PART

Pray for it
Yes
Beg for it
Til death due us part

Oh focus you treacherous heart

Appreciate the vow you made
Honor it
Desire it
Require it

Focus you treacherous heart and
Praise thinking ability

My moral code of ethics and my very
Hope for future existence

Ah yes, integrity
Elusive it would be, but for my vow

Til death...
Do us part

PROTECTOR OF MY SOUL

Soul made of dust, of matter and breath
Weak from birth regardless of mirth
Celebrated at conception, first bump, faint flutter and birth
Soul, created from love from joy and song
Power to love, to mature and have faith
in the one who deserves all worship and praise
Soul, who can choose what's good over what's bad
Who can choose life eternal in happiness and grace,
Who can choose death eternal without a small trace
Such a simple solution, such an easy resolve. Make me
do it with honor and dignity. Make me love you, be gracious
appreciative and trustworthy. Help me my God for I am
weak, not wicked but weak.

Your chosen people so rude, insolent, unthankful
and arrogant. I remember my ancestors and read of them
everyday. Why did they choose idol's, no-gods, over the living
and true God Jehovah?

Selfish not ignorant; for they knew their history well. Greedy,
and lustful, they worshiped themselves and Satan, not even
embarrassed but shouted their idolatry from the rooftops
and under the highest trees.

Oh my God, please forgive me for I have the same traits of
imperfection and sinful inclinations that plague my weak and
frustrated soul daily.

Make me do right, my God and help me have faith. Give me
your Holy Spirit and the strength to adjust my thinking and
weakness, to self restraint and justice. To think as you think
and love what you love. To hate what you hate and abhor
what is wicked in your eyes (as I must), to have your approval
and be your faithful friend. You, Jehovah, are my God and
I love you with all my heart. Please make me faithful, loyal
and true... for without you my God, there's no need for my breath.
Help me be the protector of my soul. In you I trust. I must.

RAINBOW AT MY DOOR

The wind is blowing in my hair and flowing over my skin like a cool yellow silk scarf. How refreshing after that cool light shower. Its' cool and crisp after this cleansing rain and smells of violet flowers to cover my pain.

What a beautiful sight that rainbow was and it couldn't have come at a better time.
The day started out rushed and unorganized, got to our one-day though, with time to spare.
Moved around a couple of times, got perfect seats, took off lots of heat.

Took clear concise notes and fell asleep only a few times (smile.) Time to leave, looking forward to going to Angel's house to eat and socialize with friends that I love, with husband, mother, brothers and sisters what a delight!

But

He was angry unkind and defensive: "What made you think I only wanted one sandwich for lunch today?" he said. We were almost there when I realized Caution had not been out all day. Dog! We need a doggy door, or to be more responsible maybe? No, we were just rushed that day.

He was mean, if you felt what I seen...
     "If we go back home I am not going back out!"

Grief, the dogs got to pee, naturally

That rainbow came at just the right time to organize my mind and reflect on the real purpose of life and not to absorb the strife.

RED CHILI PEPAS

Appreciation of our God given senses was enriched and encircled me as I watched a string of red chili pepper Christmas tree lights dancing on the awning of an EZ-Up shelter at Rocky Point in 2004. What a delightful breeze it was, as they swayed in the evening moonlight.

The shelter carried the most awesome delights that a person could imagine, delights that stimulate all the senses Jehovah created in us.

I thought, "if only I had lungs down to my toes," as I inhaled the pungent smells deeply arousing hunger glands from BBQ and steak, hot dogs and sausages, fish and shrimp all co-mingling in the night air, with chili, onions and garlic.

The gift of hearing, as music from all cultures rang from old school to new, from Caribbean to bop — thank you for my ears that hear those melodious sounds!

The sense of sight is a blessed delight from all the smiles that go on for miles, to watching busy brothers working and busting a glistening pungent sweet sweat.

Watching children at vigorous play, swimming in the ocean, watching schools of yellow and black striped fish playing hide and seek, floating on their bellies with teeth green from smiling in the seawater.

Yes, our senses are many. We have much to be grateful for from our thoughtful creator, our happy God.

He knew in advance how he wanted us to respond: to the awesome heavens with that cerulean blue that reflects in the ocean and causes a calming affect that makes you want to stop, suck in a deep breath of clean, pure ocean air. Makes you feel like you have lungs down to your toes, as you wiggle them in the warm soft smooth sandy beach.

Oh thank you! Jehovah my loving creator
and to think,
you have only just begun

REJOICE MY FRIENDS

For soon the desert will blossom
as the rose.

THE CHOSEN ONES

How grateful we can be when we listen to the rain and hear its gentle refrain
How grateful we can be for we are the chosen ones of Jah

We are thankful to Jah for our gifts all around that abound
  ... and abound with spiritual food that feeds us well
  ... and physical food that hunger dispels

Ah Yes,
How grateful we can be, for you see we are the Chosen Ones
The Chosen ones of our Good, our Merciful and All Mighty powerful One

We are the chosen ones of Jah

Trip

How many poems have been written about vacations?

How refreshing
How inspirational
How relaxing and oh yeah... we fell in love all over again, etc., etc., etc.,

How many poems have been written about the marvelous time they had as they
Watched the sunset
Watched the sunrise
Swam and floated in the ocean so blue,
Enjoyed the locals, the vendors, the food
the camaraderie anew... blah blah blah

How many poems have been written about

How brilliant the stars were
How luminous the moon was
And oh please, don't forget the dolphins yeah

We danced with the dolphins just five feet away from us etc., etc., etc.,

Well, as of my trip to Rocky Point with the Pipersburghs this year...

I am jealous, no longer...

Waiting On Jah

(Pr 18:10) The name of Jehovah is a strong tower. Into it the righteous runs and is given protection.

Heart, messed up and battered, weathered from the storm
I must say that my heart is swollen from sorrow

The only logical thing I can do
Is wait on Jehovah, he'll carry me though for
He's always been loyal righteous, faithful and true

WHAT HAPPENED TO US?

Ramona Wright

It's happened to me and it's happened to many
Why have we changed so much over the years
I was a happy child, carefree and chipper
I was the talented one that's what they tell me
Now I am old and tired and fat
with excess adipose tissue to bat

I can't think, I can't see, and I'm slow as molasses
I'm so slow I need help just to get to my glasses
The years have crept up on me that is no lie
The years have crept up on me I can't deny
What happened to me over time (over years)
Perhaps I can say if I look through my tears

So I turn to my God Jehovah and say
Thank you for loving us all the way
And giving us your son Jesus Christ our Savior
Yes he is the one that beseeches with speeches
To Jehovah on our behalf with love and forbearance
And to him we give thanks, for restored we will be
because we all have changed over the years

FAMILY & HOPE

Sunday, March 11, 2007
A Dear John Letter

As I listen to my little grandson cry in the other room, in the most pitiable tiny little voice, I cry with him in my heart, my soul and my spirit. I have concluded that I will work from this moment not to have anything to do with you any more John. Your lack of natural affection for your son has turned my heart to rotten refuse.

How many times have I told you to LEARN to HATE what is bad and LOVE what is good? Unkindness, lack of self-control, lack of love and natural affection for your own flesh and blood is something that will not go unnoticed by our heavenly Father Jehovah. It will never be something I can forgive. I am sick with grief and my bitter tears are unrecoverable at this point. I may see you on the other side of Armageddon if you make the necessary changes before it is too late, if you make Jehovah your own, but I do not what to see you again on this side. The pain you bring in my life is too much for me to bear son. I loved you for so many years John. I tried so very hard to teach you right from wrong, but I failed to teach you to hate what is bad and love what is good. I failed to teach you to WANT to do Jehovah's will. I know you know the difference and will not hold myself accountable any longer for your bad choices. You cannot blame me for what you are doing now. Your money cannot save us John. Your big house cannot save us during tribulation and Armageddon. Only being obedient to Jehovah TODAY and tomorrow will. ONLY you making Jehovah your own will save you from the hooks Satan has in you. I wrote the following poem in an attempt to help myself get through all this stuff you are putting me through because it is the way I feel today.

If only I could be no more. If only I could go to that deep sleep of no return, for I have failed in every respect, as a mother, grandmother and wife.

Mom

BLACK BERRY ROLLY ROLLY

Black Berry Rolly Rolly, sweetest jelly in the world, fills up your senses and makes your mouth water, makes you wanna holler, just let me put a little touch of it on a biscuit I can hardly wait.

Grandma Francis Ellen Washington, looked with fear and anxious anticipation, waiting for the Klan to leave the farm. She could feel her brothers hiding, waiting quietly in the forest, waiting for that smell on the hot black skillet, sending out the signal it's safe to come home.

Oh, how sweet the smell of burnt black berry rolly rolly! It could make their heart swell, stop the hands wrenching and the feet tapping quietly in the bush. The smell of safety, of comfort. *It's clear to come home boys.* No one can catch you, molest you or turn you into strange fruit tonight brothers.

Oh mighty black iron skillet bring us home, home to the warmth of a fire burning softly in the old black pot belly stove. Old crusty black skillet that holds the power of life and death, lay your juice on us tonight, girl. Come sweet smell, come on! Come on the wind, hurry on up now. Oh hurry please, come on down so our nostrils can inhale your sweet smell of freedom, of comfort, laughter, safety and family. Yep, black berry rolly rolly sizzlin' and smoking up through the night air, come on and save us from this cold black night. Bring us on home one more time. One more night.

BLACK IRON SKILLETS

Iron skillets have been a powerful tool in the hands of black women thru out the past two hundred years of history and longer.
Maybe that's why you always find they are heavy, tempered, beautiful and black. You find them usually either full of good things to eat (bringing contentment and joy making life a delight,) or filled with death, sorrow and treachery.

Let's take a journey of the iron skillet handed down to me from my great-great-grandmother, who would pour the juice of black berry jam on her pot belly stove to signal her brothers (who were ministers during slavery time,) that it was safe to come home. It was against the law to teach slaves to read, but her brothers would do it anyway, using the Bible as the teaching tool. Eventually they, one-and-all, became *strange fruit**, but the teaching gene has continued in the family to this day, and the love and loyalty for and of our Creator still thrives.

*Meaning they were lynched.

GANGSTER PHILOSOPHY

Gangster Philosophy Mentality, Brutality, and Philosophy has paralyzed the family and brought
about a new way of thinking to those who are the keepers of the minds
They walk the streets with no fear
Sagging pants and drinking beer
The life of a gangster is short
Because you never know when you'll get caught
Their reality, their mentality is they didn't do nothin, see nothin, hear nothin
Nothing but sit around and drink beer, smoking weed
I didn't do nothin. Well that's the truth, for in reality you didn't do nothing for your
Mothers, fathers, grandmothers and grandfathers, aunts and uncles, cousins, sisters and brothers.
All are dealing with your Gangster Mentality. We are supposed to be the Keeper of the Minds, but
what can you do, when their minds are pretentious and unkind, blind
Gangster Mentality Hears no Evil, Sees no Evil, But you sure can speak some evil
Gangster mentality: you didn't see it so it didn't happen
Don't talk about it
Don't think about it
Am I supposed to just pretend nothing happened because nothing happened?
Did you see him take that shot and pass the pot?
No I didn't see that Sir
So, don't repeat something you didn't see and if you did see it
Pretend as if nothing happened because nothing happened
What do I mean nothing happened?
Nothing happened
Nothing happened
So when do I actually deal with it all?
When my child's gang rivals come to the house and shoot it up
When my child's gang rivals come to the house and kill his or her siblings, cousins and whoever
else is visiting in my house?
When do I actually deal with it?
When does it become my reality?
When I have to work overtime to earn extra money
My hard earned money to put on his books so that someone he borrowed from in prison won't jack
him up or kill him?
When do I actually deal with it?
When does it become my reality?
Every Single Day!

A song of parental dismay and loss

IF ONLY

If only I could be no more. If only I could go to that deep sleep of no return, for I have failed in every respect, as a mother, grandmother and wife

I ask myself in my deep despair
Why can't she be a millionaire
Why can't she be a billionaire
Why can't she be your wife, my son
Why is she my son's baby's momma
Why is she like a daughter to me

Why does she seem like the perfect one I would have chosen for a daughter-in-law

Why is her past an issue, He knew her past when he choose her

Why is her love for my son an issue, he wanted her, choose her and made her fall in love with him

Was it a game, only to kick her aside because she wasn't bringing in the money
Was it only to get his best friend's girl, as his best friend took his wife. Could he pull her?
Was it only to test and see if he could even have a baby. Not caring that this tiny life is now a lifelong responsibility

Why is Josiah an issue, my son wanted him, asked for him and
Together they created him in love, but in the end... Where is the Love?
Only she delivered
Only she came through
She didn't have to have him
She didn't have to give birth, for Josiah could have been flushed, just matter in the dust
It was a miracle that he was even conceived, because Josiah's mother womb was damaged as a child

All things considered, it was Adam, not Eve that Jehovah looked to save, his wife and all his seed

It was Adam that brought death to all his children, including us today
It was Adam that passed the buck when he sinned and blamed the very God that created, loved and protected him; "It was that Woman YOU gave me" he said, "that is why I sinned"

That was a lie, for Jehovah would never do anything to hurt us

IF ONLY (CON'T)

Unless, Josiah's father turns to Jehovah his God
Josiah will be no more
Unless Meleigha turns to Jehovah our God
Josiah will be no more
Why is her family so wonderful
Why did they have to be a part of my heart so soon
Why can't they be awful and someone I can't stand
Why is my grandson so beautiful
Why is my grandson so perfect
Why is my grandson the love of my life
Why do I feel like my son is so wrong
Why do I feel like my son is so heartless
Why do I feel like my son has hurt my heart

Because of the love HE has of money! why do I feel the stabs of pain all over,
the tears and the fears have made my world (filled with treachery and
grief, a place I no longer wish to exist
If only I could close my eyes and wake up in the new system
If only I could close my eyes and make everything right
I cannot do that, so feel worthless... the misery so overwhelming to contend
The pain was hard enough when I lost my daughters Sylvia, Tonya and Lisa
The pain is more than I can bear, now that I have lost John, my first-born son and his baby's
momma

The pain was hard enough when I lost my granddaughters Sterling, Silver and Sloane
The pain is more than I can bear, now that I have lost my first-born grandsons Elijah, Josiah
& great grandson Kyle

But I will recover from this loss my God has promised me, not to even remember the
sweetness of their company. If only I could close my eyes and be no more.
At least in the sweet peace of death I feel no pain. I feel no grief.

Of course, this is not my choice, as I do not belong to me. I belong to Jehovah and he says
no, my life is his and precious as it can be. He says I can endure; even to death, and even
though I long for it and wish I had that peace, and cure to this deep gash of pain, I know he
will fill my heart with comfort, love, and harmony once again.

A song of parental dismay and loss

In Spite of My Dear Mother
In Spite of Your Dear Mother
Love Jehovah God My Children

No my dear children, I don't serve Jehovah because my mother was brilliant and read the Dead Sea Scrolls — the same woman that allowed my father to rape my sister with no consequence.

I serve Jehovah in spite of my mother

I don't serve Jehovah because my mother told me Jehovah is the true God, that it is the Whole Obligation of mankind to worship him in spirit and truth — the same mother that allowed my father to give me gonorrhea at the age of five.

I serve Jehovah in spite of my mother

I didn't choose to dedicate my life to Jehovah because my mother said that is the least I could do since he lovingly bought me out of slavery to sin and death with the very blood of his first born son from the hands of my grandparents who sold me to Satan. The same mother that allowed my stepfather to beat and molest my baby brothers.

I serve Jehovah in spite of my mother

No my dear children, I say from my heart I do not Serve the God of the universe, The God of Love, The God that Causes to Become, because of the mother that bore me and listened in the back room while my ex held a gun to my head in her living room waiting to see if I lived or died that night.

I serve him, in spite of my mother

Babies of mine, look past your treacherous deceitful tricky hearts, search for the true God, Worship Jehovah with Spirit and Truth

Serve Jehovah in spite of YOUR mother, who was a liar, a thief and prostitute. Use your clear thinking ability, your intellectual reasoning and see the simple uncomplicated truth that Jehovah provides to those that truly desire the truth, not watered down, not covered with fluff and whipped cream.

... LOVE JEHOVAH GOD MY CHILDREN (CON'T)

Serve Jehovah In spite of your mother, who carried a 45 and tried to kill her first husband with bullets flying unaware that she may have killed her three little girls. Who murdered her 6ᵗʰ child a baby boy of 7 pounds, listened as he cried and turned her head to the left.

Jehovah calls to you, he wishes to give you treasure worth more than gold and silver. He wishes to give you wisdom, and knowledge that will lead to your eternal happiness and bliss, he begs you to test him out and see if he won't pour into your laps all that is good.

Serve Jehovah in spite of your mother, who many times was unfaithful to the very God she begs you to adore.

Listen to the wisdom of your mother who was unable to set a perfect example, don't be fools for you ALL know the beginning of wisdom is the fear of Jehovah. Wisdom and discipline are what fools hate. Love what is good, Hate what is Bad. Read the Bible daily. Return to your God and serve Jehovah with spirit and truth.

Serve Jehovah in spite of your mother who survived long enough to see her children grow to adults and daily reaps the consequences of her stupid choices.

For now, our family is split, we are on two sides of the universal issue. Jehovah does have the right to tell us how to live our lives and gives us free will to choose which side we support. We are not better off, physically, mentally, emotionally or spiritually, DOING IT OUR OWN WAY as Satan claimed to Eve and all the angels in heaven. Jehovah is not interested in, nor will he accept worship that is forced or coerced by parents or loved ones, therefore study and see clearly the reasons why we should love him, learn to love him and he will love you forever. Even his heavenly hosts saw that. Any imperfect mother would want her children to be good or obedient because they love her and know she has their best interest at heart and so does Jehovah. Satan's challenge that we only serve Jah for what we get is a lie. Job proved that. This issue has been proved a million times. Mankind cannot rule themselves with justice and love. 6,000 years of human government has proved that. Satan's religions have proved wicked, evil and selfish, blessing the very weapons that murder

... LOVE JEHOVAH GOD MY CHILDREN (CON'T)

and kill themselves over land and money. Jehovah is the True God and even though imperfect be his followers. We refuse to go to war and kill each other out of LOVE for Jehovah our God and our fellow man. That Is a clear Identifying mark of true Religion.

Soon, everyone not serving Jehovah, will turn on his faithful followers and try to wipe us off the face of the earth. Will I see my children pointing me out one day, or secretly putting my name on the hit list? Odds and Satan say Yes, I may live to see that day. My Hope and Prayer is that, they will choose to serve Jehovah out of Love for the truth and righteousness. How Jesus' heart must have hurt when he looked into Peter's eyes when he denied him that day. I pray that my children will believe the truth, not the philosophical filth of mankind, be it Aristotle or the current great Teachers of the 20th century. But the 40, Shepherds, doctors, fisherman, lawyers and fig nippers who over 1,600 years were inspired by Jehovah God to write and protect the Bible as his precious gift to mankind. The very book that will teach you how to gain everlasting life in peace and happiness.

Please my loved ones, I beg you my children, Serve Jehovah in Spite Of Your Mother's poor example, poor choices and hundreds of imperfections.

Dedicated to All Children with Imperfect Parents

MAMMA
Love Jordan Reynolds Lofton Valadez

Her ashes at the bottom of the San Francisco Bay Bridge or flowing in Seas all over the world, loyally awaiting re-creation
Still the powerful, spiritual, black woman in my life. Still the woman I love and admire
Still the woman I try to inspire
The woman who gave me everything I value in life
The woman who gave me music, dance, poetry and Jah
The woman who gave me love, joy or pain... my choice of course
The woman with whom I shared the sunshine and rainbows
Who gave me the arts and love of just being
Of seeing, of loyalty, faithfulness and desire for something better, of the very best that is available for those that just see it, the little things that are so big
Of scenarios in all of their glory
Of cynicism and not just the gory
500 books she read before five
Mensa sought her only to be laughed at with a smirk on her lips and a toss of her head, "Come on now really," she said, "just how smart is that?"
Brilliant as the Sun, Strong as Diamonds, Talented, Beautiful
Sought after by famous men for her talent no, they couldn't impress her, or afford her.
"Can they give me everlasting life?" she said, "Never to grow old or get sick, never be bored or unhappy? Can they give me perfection in mind, body and spirit with positive interactions and friends never to depart? Diamonds and pearls in my hand to examine, to experiment with and use to our ecological advantage? What about security, no crime, no hunger sickness or death? If not, why bother with their offer, they can't afford me" she said.
Not this Tower of Power
"Who needs them?" she said.
Not her, not with her charm, her wit, her brain. Not her with fortitude, beauty and grace, her face. Not this Tower of Power who survived and thrived in a madman driven world, where women were considered decoration or perversion
Not this Powerful, Spiritual, Black Woman.
Not This Tower.

MY BABY BOY IS HOME AT LAST
BUT A BABY HE IS NO MORE

My son's home, after five years of tears and fears, turbulent heartache and confusion, disillusionment and pain, but the pain stops here! As joy and help is on the way from the man that was once a boy. A boy full of himself has blossomed into a man we can depend on, a man trustworthy and loyal, true to his God and faith. A man that is worth the wait. Thank you my God for bringing him home to his mother's and father's arms. Thank you Jehovah for your patience and grace, his sins, your son can erase. For all eternity I thank you from the bottom of my heart and continue my prayers for his continued success in his race for life in your loving arrangement. May your son, continue to intervene on our behalf and lovingly, comfort us as we continue our prays and vigil for the rest of my children to come to their senses and welcome your love into their hearts. For you and you alone are our God, the one who loves us, and cherishes us, feeds us spiritually and physically and wants us to live forever in peace and happiness. You are the happy God and I love you Jehovah with all my heart, mind and soul.

MY MOTHER'S CHILDREN

My mother's children were loved and cherished we five
From Jewel the first born to David the last
Yep I must say we sure had a blast
We danced, and we laughed, we cried and bounced back
For our mother loved us the best she knew how
Now she wasn't perfect, made many mistakes, in judgment and
choices (some I truly hate)
but she truly loved us in spite of all her smarts
Yes she truly loved us with all of her heart

STERLING SLEEPING

What beauty, what a gem.
This graceful beauty should always be here
to love, to laugh, and chase butterflies, with
her children, her husband and ancestors.
For life as promised by Jehovah for all
eternity, if she chooses him with all loyalty.
For Jah is a good God, the one and only
true God. He loves her and cherishes the
dedication she made, perhaps in haste but
truly from the heart. It's not too late to re-
prioritize your list, put Jah first, and joy you
will find. For you are a gem, with grace and
beauty, not just from the outside, but deep
in your heart. So dear baby girl, now a
woman, mature and with clarity, make a
fresh start. Always from the heart.

Grandma Mona

THE POWER OF A CHILD

Young man, young woman do you fully appreciate the power you posses
Power to bring peace in a home torn apart by deception and grief
Power to bring hope refreshment and love
Power to bring smiles to a broken spirit
Power to bring back the love that was stolen away secretly in the night
Power to restore faith in the mother who bore you, loved you, carried you in her protective womb
Faith that you will not stay in the tomb
Power to show The Friends that they're wrong about you; No, I am not so insecure, so selfish that I make my mom sad, disrespect her, neglect her, frustrate and abate her
No, I am not so foolish that I entertain my peers with sneers and jeers of disdain and bad jokes that they laugh at to keep me from their throat or
Bully them into submission, knowing I really just want them to like me
You have God given power at birth to refresh and restore to bring comfort and joy
For all to explore

WEEDS🐦

It's amazing how much I don't understand their lack of love. It's amazing that I care one minute and could care less the next. It's frustrating and painful and humiliating that I want their love, so much — their commendation and approval.

Why do I crave the approval of a mist that is here today and gone today! Of grass that withers and dries, that's heartless and unresponsive to my gentle touch, my tender heart, my deep abiding love.

I shower those stinking weeds with my tears with no response, so I must stop and leave them to blow away in the wind that Jah created. He knows best what to do with weeds. My salty, imperfect, human tears will only further their eventual deterioration and decay. Only Jah knows what to do with weeds. He can choose what he wills with them for I cannot judge hearts, only reactions from my efforts. Jah has the power and wisdom to judge those hearts, their motives, desires and the fires they ignite.

He it is who will determine whether any weed, living now or in the past, is worth a resurrection or recreation of life eternal, or to just let them go tumbling on. I can only pray that Jah does not think me a weed and work hard to rectify my imperfections and deceit. For in reality, who am I but a drop in the bucket of this magnificent cosmos Jah created?

Thank goodness Jehovah's heart is bigger than mine, for in myself, I only see only the makings of fertilizer as an asset to this magnificent earth to help continue in the cycles Jehovah started. Jehovah's heart is bigger than my heart and sees so much more. Only Jehovah knows my heart if I'm loyal or not.

Ahhhhh! How comforting! Now I know what to work on next, the weeds in my own heart.

WORDS

(Pr 18:21) 21 Death and life are in the power of the tongue, and he that is loving it will eat its fruitage.

My mother told me when I was a child that words have the power of life and
Death. That my very own words could actually get me killed one day if I wasn't careful, and
thoughtful and respected the power they contain. Zip your lips tight, she said, and let those
words play in your brain. Control them, organize them, synchronize them and then carefully,
slowly, let them flow like beautiful butterflies all in a row from your pretty sweet little lips.
I was only six or seven years old at that time.

I can't remember what I said that would create a need for her to tell me that in my jaws, my
words, my throat, and my tongue lie the power of life and death — my own at that!
Maybe it was that little girl next door who I told there was no real Santa Clause, that he was a
lie, a myth and fable, 'cause where was the chimney he was to come down in the Projects?
And how come there are so many Santa's on every other corner each year, begging for
money and drunk most of the time as I recall, and so did she... Ah, that little girl of three!

I am 58 years old now; half a century seems like a long time a lifetime but it's not!
It's not even a drop in the bucket of time. I need forever to make him mine.
For I have hurt my dearly beloved, my words have caused pain, so much so, that he can't
stand next to me without looking, hoping wishing he never met me...

I truly believe the scripture that says an answer when mild turns away rage. The article I read
said that words cause pain. And even if spoken calmly will, can, and have inflamed.

Inflamed so much so, that now I say — in all sincerity — please no insults. No sarcasm or put-
downs. Not in my jaws, my throat, on my tongue, not in my mouth. For my mother told me
when I was a child that words have power. The power of life and death and could get me
killed one day.

Fɪɴ

ABOUT THE AUTHOR

Born in 1948, in Los Angeles, California, Ramona Lofton Wright's earliest memories are of sitting at her mother's feet watching and singing as her mother tapped on the pedals of the piano while playing Mozart, Chopin or boogie-woogie. Ramona recalls the delicate, miniature porcelain slippers her mother fired in a red brick kiln located in the basement of the family home in Prescott, Arizona (her family's homestead since the late 1800's).

Ramona's love of painting began over five decades ago in kindergarten. The instructor gave the students an assignment to paint a picture of a large bowl of fruit situated in the middle of the classroom. Ramona watched the other children, and observed that their grapes were small and beady, their bananas were skinny and shriveled, and their apples did not look very appetizing. She set her goal. She painted big, juicy, purple, grapes; fat, shiny, yellow bananas; deep, ruby-red, apples and plump, happy, oranges. Her entire worksheet overflowed with ripe, succulent fruit. The teacher walked among the students offering critique and encouragement. She stopped at Ramona's painting. With a twinkle in her eye she exclaimed, "Ramona, this fruit looks good enough to eat!" She accomplished her immediate goal and to this day, approaches her painting with that same childhood desire to bring something tantalizing, delicious and beautiful from her palette to the table of her canvas for all to enjoy.

Drawing on personal experience and a diverse family heritage, it is Ramona's desire to translate her passion for life, a gift she inherited from her mother Love Jordan Valadéz, into her paintings. As a youngster her mother noticed her talent and took her to many art classes. In elementary school, Ramona played marbles in exchange for paper so she could draw. She never had enough paper. Her first painting of note was an oil of a Kachina doll. She won 1st prize at the Los Angeles State Fair; what an exciting day for the whole family! In Jr. high school she would draw horses and pencil sketches of students for lunch money. She learned a terrible lesson when she drew a picture of a young lady with an extremely large nose. Everyone said it looked just like her but the student would not pay the dollar because her nose was too long. Needless to say, she went hungry that day. She studied at Scottsdale Community College under David Sylar and Professor Dyer. As an adult, the family structure changed, necessitating that she stop painting and take a day job. For over 20 years she worked at Arizona Public Service Company. She has shown at the APS Museum in downtown Phoenix. She retired when her mother became ill with cancer. She and her sisters took care of their mother in Ramona's home until she died. She inherited her mother's art supplies, books, easels and paint. Slowly, she picked up the brushes and knew she would never again put them down. Ramona's medium is watercolor, pastels and acrylics. She lives with her husband of 24 years, Joseph Wright and paints from her studio "Fine Art Done Wright Galleries" in Phoenix, AZ. Ramona and Joseph have 12 children, 12 grandchildren and 1 great grand.

www.ingramcontent.com/pod-product-compliance
Lightning Source LLC
Chambersburg PA
CBHW041503280526
45792CB00004B/1111